NORTH CAROLINA

Featuring the Photography of Chris Swan
CLB 1255
© 1985 Illustrations and text: Colour Library Books Ltd.,
   Guildford, Surrey, England.
Text filmsetting by Acesetters Ltd., Richmond, Surrey, England.
Printed in Spain.
All rights reserved.
1985 edition published by Crescent Books, distributed by Crown Publishers, Inc.
ISBN 0 517 456230
h g f e d c b a

NORTH CAROLINA

Text by
ANN McCARTHY

Designed & Produced by
TED SMART and DAVID GIBBON

CRESCENT BOOKS
NEW YORK

Sir Walter Raleigh was granted a charter by Queen Elizabeth I, allowing him to explore and colonize "remote heathen and barbarous lands" not already owned by a Christian prince. Raleigh – soldier, courtier, historian and poet – had great charm, which he used at will. He was handsome, tall – over six foot – and slender. His curly, brown hair was brushed back and ornamented with double rows of pearls. He had a trim, pointed beard, a brown, upswept mustache and expressive gray eyes. In Elizabethan court circles he was not overlooked. In fact, he gained the Queen's favor, and with it the right to explore.

In 1584 he dispatched two ships to the North American coast. On July 13 of that year a party landed in North Carolina, somewhere near Roanoke Island, and saw "the goodliest land under the cope of heaven." Captain Barlowe, one of the leaders thought "in all the world the like abundance is not to be found." He described it as the "most pleasant and fertile ground, replenished with goodly Cedars, and divers other sweete woods, full of Corrants, flaxe, and many other notable commodities." He also mentioned that they had encountered "gentle, loving, and faithful" Indians.

Just behind this expedition another, comprised of 108 persons including geographer Thomas Hariot and the artist John White, settled on Roanoke Island. Within a year they had antagonized the loving and faithful Indians. It seemed judicious to accept a ride home with Sir Francis Drake, who was passing by. Soon after their departure in June, 1586, Sir Richard Grenville, cousin to Sir Walter, found the settlement deserted; and, being "unwilling to lose the possession of the country," he left fifteen men on Roanoke Island with provisions for two years.

The following summer some 150 colonists, led by Governor John White, landed at Roanoke. Their destination was Chesapeake Bay, with its fertile land, deep-water harbor and friendly Chesepian Indians. Stopping first off the North Carolina coast, the fleet's master, Simon Ferinando, irritated with the Governor throughout the voyage, refused to sail further. The colonists remained at Roanoke Island. And here, on August 18, 1857, Governor White's granddaughter

Virginia Dare was born. She was christened Virginia in honor of the new territory.

Somewhere near the earlier settlements they had begun building homes. But trouble flared with the peace-loving Croatoan Indians and their chief Manteo, who intercepted an attack which was meant for the Roanoke Indians. Governor White patched up the short-lived problem, as least so he thought, and turned to the issue of a supply shortage. He returned to England for help, leaving instructions that if the settlers moved "they should not faile to write or carve on the trees or posts of the dores the name of the place where they should be seated." And if they were forced to flee, a Maltese cross was to be added above the letters.

Because of a series of obstacles, three years passed before White returned to the New World. On August 18, 1590 – his granddaughter's third birthday – he waded ashore at Roanoke Island and found no one. The settlers had vanished completely. After searching the island he discovers the word "CRO" carved in a tree. Farther inland, overgrown with weeds and vines, he located the palisaded enclosure where the people had lived. On a post to the right of the entrance "and 5. foote from the ground in fayre Capotall letters was graven CROATOAN without any crosse or signe of distresse." Goods were scattered about, including "bookes torne from the covers," rusted armor, and "Mappes rotten and spoyled with rayne."

Before the fleet could cast off, a storm nearly wrecked the ships. The captains, wary of storms in the treacherous waters off Cape Hatteras, just south of Roanoke Island, and more interested in capturing Spanish treasure than rescuing colonists, sailed for the Caribbean. White, only a few miles from Croatoan, as the Cape was called in those days, had no choice but to go with them. He never returned. "I would to God my wealth were answerable to my will," he wrote sadly of his abandoned hopes to see his colony and family.

Four centuries of speculation have followed the disappearance of the Lost Colony. What happened to Virginia Dare, the first child of English parents born in the New World, and to the rest of that settlement? Did the Indians or Spanish slaughter them? Did they drown trying to go back to England? Did they live among the Indians and intermarry? Through John White's writings and watercolors we have pieces of the story, but no one has the definitive answer.

The voyagers of 1585 and 1587 landed on the north end of Roanoke Island. Near that spot today are the Elizabethan Gardens, the Waterside Theatre and Fort Raleigh National Historic Site. The site conserves the earthworks of the 1585 fort and the Elizabethan Gardens mingle informal plantings with 16th-century formal gardens. Meandering paths protected by oaks and magnolias are fringed with azaleas, lilies, crepe myrtle and summer bedding plants. Then, at sunset, Waterside Theatre presents America's oldest outdoor drama, "The Lost Colony." In 1937 Paul Green premiered his "symphonic drama" on the shores of Roanoke Sound.

Today, Roanoke Island and the crescent sliver of the Outer Banks are summer vacation spots. Tides of tourists visit Kill Devil Hills and Kitty Hawk, the testing ground for the Wright Brothers' airborne vehicles. Just south of the first flying fields is Nags Head, which reputedly earned its name when residents tied lanterns on the necks of their horses and rode up and down the dunes luring ships into the shoals, where they were held to be fair prey for looting.

The Atlantic coast sweeps down from the Virginia capes in a series of arcs. This edge of land called the Outer Banks is a thin ribbon of sandy islands separated from the mainland by shallow bays and sounds. At the southern tip of the first arc is Cape Hatteras, whose treacherous waters conceal offshore shoals and are called the "graveyard of the Atlantic." To assuage the deluge of shipwrecks the world's tallest lighthouse was erected there in 1848 and rebuilt in 1872. Five sailing vessels were smashed in the vicinity during the final days of its completion alone. The lighthouse is 163 feet high and throws a 160,000-candlepower beam visible for 19 miles. The area above Hatteras is called Cape Hatteras National Seashore. Ducks, geese, plovers, sandpipers, gulls, terns and skimmers and, occasionally, white swans flock by the thousands to feed along its marshes and 128 miles of public beaches. Foxes, racoons, muskrats, shrews and squirrels live on the land. Marlin, billfish and bass populate its waters. Cape Lookout National Seashore is south of Hatteras. Over 500 vessels have sunk off the tip of Cape Lookout since 1585.

On the sand beach where the tide ebbs and flows is a whole underwater world. The surf is frequently filled with fish less than an inch long. Blue crabs scavenge on the bottom. Just seaward of low tide live flounder, sand dollars, sea cucumbers and several species of clams and shellfish. Porpoises are often seen riding above the waves and plunging beneath the surface.

On the dry-sand part of the beach, above the reach of the high tide, are the round burrows of the ghost crab. Here is found the first vegetation – hardy, salt-tolerant grasses such as sea rocket and sea oats. Sometimes standing as tall as a basketball player, the fluffy, straw-colored grasses are as elegant as egret plumes. The sea oat contributes more than beauty, however. Its expansive root system spreads under the surface of the beach and anchors sand that would shift, laying the foundations of the dune.

The Chowan River estuary is second in size, on the East Coast, only to Chesapeake Bay. Its protected waters and marshland grasses make it an important fishery resource. Shrimp, oysters, blue crab, hard clams, and bay scallops are harvested by North Carolina fishermen.

Okracoke Island lies between Cape Hatteras and Cape Lookout. A quiet bay near Okracoke village is known as "Teach's Hole" because it was the hiding place of the pirate "Blackbeard" (Edward Teach), killed there in 1718.

Back in the early 1700s it wasn't so terrible for men to seize a few "prizes" from other ships. In fact, during wartime it was legal to go privateering. Once the war was over it was hard to slip back into mundane seafaring. The people of the Carolina shore towns seemed to understand the pirate's predicament. Besides, the men who took their small, shallow-draft crafts across the sounds, through an inlet, into the Atlantic to pilfer passing merchantmen, brought back welcome goods to an impoverished colony. The goods sold far below the price of legal merchandise. Pirates were often an isolated community's best asset.

However, piracy didn't remain in check. There was a shortage of "gentlemen pirates" like Major Stede Bonnet, a former British officer from a respected family. Many were cruel and their cruelty cumulated in Blackbeard. He was the terror of the North Carolina coast, not only because of his blood-thirsty deeds, but also because of his appearance. He was 6 feet 4 inches tall, weighed 250 pounds and had wild, red-rimmed eyes and dark skin. His shaggy, black hair was long, and his beard was braided and tied with multi-colored ribbons. He often soaked long hemp cord strings in a solution of saltpeter and lime water. When he put the strings in his ears and lit them, wisps of green-colored smoke curled around his head. Across his chest, in a bandolier, he carried three braces of pistols which were ready for instant firing. More pistols, daggers and cutlasses were strapped around his waist with a bright sash. He was indomitable as he cruised along the shores of Pamlico Sound, capturing ships. A man wrote to his friend that Blackbeard "was of the most bloody disposition, and cruel to brutality; his name became Terror; some Governors being remiss to pursuing him, he almost put a stop to the trade of several... colonies." But Blackbeard met his match in Captain Maynard, who, after an attack by Blackbeard, ordered his men to feign death. At just the right time Maynard's "dead" crew came to life. Blackbeard and

Maynard came face to face. Loaded with gun shot, and with a slash in the neck, Blackbeard finally fell to the deck. With one more shot, he was dead. Maynard ordered two of his men to cut off Blackbeard's head and hang it on the ship's bow as a trophy and a warning to other pirates.

Below Okracoke and across Core Sound from Cape Lookout is Beaufort, North Carolina's third oldest town. Beaufort still retains the charm and flavor of an 18th-century coastal town. Rows of spreading oaks and elms frame narrow, curving streets. The old houses, meticulously built by ships' carpenters, imitate a style seen by early mariners in the Bahamas – a sloping roof extends without a break to cover the front porch. Wooden-steepled churches, surrounded by cemeteries with weather-worn monuments, appear much as they did over a century ago. Facing the inlet, Beaufort is a fishing port, resort and trade town. Both menhaden and food fish are caught and processed here and at nearby Morehead City. Though not eaten, menhaden is the state's most valuable fish, yielding oil for many uses including soaps, lipsticks, paints and for livestock feed. The fishing boats with crow's nests or lookout stations are a distinctive trademark of the Beaufort waterfront. The making of conical nets by hand is another industry unique to this region.

North Carolina's seaside resorts are on narrow islands that are bordered by both ocean and sound. Moored at fishing villages are large cabin cruisers and commercial fishing boats. There are beaches for swimming and surfcasting, and picnic areas among the dunes. Across the inlet is Fort Macon, with recreational features and a classic, early-nineteenth-century military fort. It was seized by the Confederate forces in 1861, and taken by the Union forces the following year. Preserved as part of a park area in 1924, Fort Macon was called back into active service for a few years during World War II. It is a historic landmark today and houses a small museum.

South of Fort Macon and past Topsail and Surf City for some three hundred miles a water route threads its way through rivers and sounds. The surf along the southeastern beaches is more gentle and warmer than that along the Outer Banks. Sailing is a popular sport at Wrightsville Beach, one of North Carolina's oldest resorts.

Wilmington, chief city in the Cape Fear Country, offers a plethora of friendly residents, exceptional architecture, historical neighborhoods and nearby beaches. Southern hospitality, with an emphasis on entertaining in homes rather than public places, is an important feature of Wilmington, and its architecture, with many examples of the Greek Revival style, is legendary. Native son, TV's David Brinkley says, "It may be a startling fact, but true – Wilmington has a greater number of interesting houses than Williamsburg, Virginia. We don't have as much history, but we have architecture."

Since its beginning as a river port city in the 1730s, shipyards have lined Wilmington's waterfront. Skeletal remains from other eras still speckle the shore. Toward the end of the Civil War Wilmington became the Confederacy's most important seaport, shipping cotton and serving the naval stores industry. Eventually manufacturing and lumber came to the fore, but the Cotton Exchange, a restored riverfront area, bears witness to the time when cotton was king and steamboats were sovereign. The complex, with over 30 specialty shops and restaurants, refurbished old brick buildings and ballast stone courtyards, covers an entire downtown block. It housed Alexander Sprunt & Son's cotton export company, one of the biggest in the world. The four-story Boney-Harper Milling Company has manufactured grits, hominy and corn meal since 1884. Saloons for mariners and a boarding house were in adjoining buildings.

Inland from the piers Wilmington's Gothic spired historic houses rise above trees and gardens much as they did in the 18th and 19th centuries. Scattered horse troughs, hitching posts, iron gates and fences are reminders of those past days. The panoply of period styles offers an in-depth study of architecture. The Doric, Ionic and Corinthian columns and pilasters on the Greek Revival homes, as well as the characteristics of Italianate, Gothic and Queen Anne, are seen throughout the city. Porticos, piazzas and canopy porches; gambrel, hip and mansard roofs; dentils and finials; sawnwork and stickwork; frieze vents, brackets, cornices, quoins and cupolas – all contribute to the charm of the eclectic architecture.

A sampling of the Historic Wilmington Tour begins with the Burgwin-Wright House. The colonial gentleman's townhouse was built in 1771. In April 1781 after the Battle of Guilford Court House, British Lord Cornwallis and his stafff occupied the house because it was the finest in the area. Its three-story kitchen is an outbuilding overlooking a boxwood and flower garden. In the next block the Zebulon Laimer House, an opulent example of Italian Revival architecture, has been home to Latimer descendants for 112 years. Along the river, the Governor Dudley Mansion, built in 1825, was home of the state's first elected governor, and Thalian Hall, a restored 19th-century community theater, is still presenting stage productions.

Only 10 miles away the Atlantic Ocean, with its bordering beaches, is the backdrop for neighboring communities. Wrightsville Beach, Kure Beach, Carolina Beach, and others north to Topsail Island and south to Southport and Oak Island, supply enough sand for swarms of sunbathers. North Carolina's coastal climate means most sports can be enjoyed all year round. Midway between New York and Florida, in Cape Fear Country, surfers ride the waves, sailors race in regattas, and fishermen win Marlin Tournaments. The Cape Fear Rugby Club offers strenuous exercise and a spring and fall playing schedule for university students and area businessmen.

Closer to home, the Cape Fear River is responsible for Wilmington's growth and change. The river was first explored in 1524 by Giovanni da Verrazano, representing the King of France. Verrazano described what he saw as "...open Country rising in height above the sandie shoare with many faire fields and plaines, full of mighty great woods, some very thicke, as pleasant and delectable to behold, as is possible to imagine."

Discovery did not mean settlement. Cape Fear area's first colony was established in 1725 on the west bank of the river, some 14 miles inland. Brunswick Town succumbed to attacks by the Spanish and then the British, not surviving much beyond the American Revolution. But, north of Brunswick Town, is a lasting monument called Orton Plantation. On lands granted by the Lords Proprietors, "King" Roger Moore cultivated a rice plantation and capped it with a magnificent manor house. Orton is represented in a mural on the dining room wall of Blair House in Washington, D.C., guest house for visiting officials and heads of state. Originally built in 1730, with additions in 1840 and 1910, Orton is considered to be an outstanding example of antebellum architecture. Visitors can walk through gardens of oaks, magnolias, cypress, pine trees, azaleas, camellias as well as other rare ornamental plants.

About 20 miles west of Wilmington in Pender County is Moores Creek Battlefield, a national historic site. There, on February 27, 1776, the first Revolutionary War battle in North Carolina was fought and won by the patriots. In the war between the states, Fort Fisher guarded the entrance to the Cape Fear River for blockade runners on their way to and from Wilmington. The blockade runners furnished the last supply line for the Confederacy. Fort Fisher's soldiers resisted the Federal troops until January 1865, when the fort fell in the largest land and sea battle of the war up until that time. An estimated 50 warships assaulted the fort for 48 hours, forcing the Confederates to withdraw and turning the tide against the Southern cause.

It's fun to take the ferry from Fort Fisher across the Cape Fear River to Southport. During the hour-long excursion you may pass oil tankers or container ships bearing international flags, red and black tugboats pushing behemoth barges, seagulls catching pieces of tourists, bread on the fly, shad fishermen in dwarfed boats, and, on occasion, you may see draw bridges expand to allow the passage of ships' superstructures.

At Southport you can see the creek where "Gentleman Pirate" Stede Bonnett is said to have hidden his pirate ship and was eventually captured. The picturesque seaport is lined with charming homes and time-worn fishing boats.

Up the coast at the confluence of the Neuse and Trent rivers sits New Bern, the second oldest city in North Carolina. Like so many North Carolina towns, New Bern's charm is in the preservation of its past. Massive brick town houses, stately Georgian residences and Wisteria-laden clapboard cottages rim narrow streets shaded by oaks, poplars elms and pecan. Many of the streets are still paved with the original brickwork.

New Bern, named for Switzerland's city of Berne, was settled first by Swiss Baron Christopher de Graffenreid in 1710. He was given £4,000 by Queen Anne of England and bought 17,5000 acres from the eight Lords Proprietors. In 1663 and 1665 Charles II had granted them the territory that is now North and South Carolina. The grants were to show the King's gratitude to leaders who had helped him when he was in exile. They gave the Lords Proprietors tremendous power. De Graffenreid also paid King Taylor, Tuscarora Indian Chief and John Lawson, the Surveyor General, for the land. The town was laid out with the streets "in the form of a cross, one arm extending from river to river, and the other, from the point, back indefinitely."

In September 1711, Lawson, who was friendly with the Indians, took de Graffenreid on a trip up the Neuse River to explore the land to the west of New Bern. A band of Tuscarora Indians captured them. After a lengthy debate among the tribal leaders, they tortured Lawson to death and freed de Graffenreid, agreeing to spare his colony at New Bern if he promised not to retaliate when they attacked. As the sun rose on September 22, the Tuscaroras led their raid, leaving New Bern untouched but killing farmers all along the Neuse and Pamlico rivers. De Graffenreid tried to keep his promise not to fight, but the colonists took up arms. New Bern was no longer spared. The Tuscaroras finally surrendered, but de Graffenreid's settlement was devastated. In 1713 many of them returned to Switzerland.

Proprietor Governor Col. Thomas Pollock picked up the pieces at New Bern, and in 1723 it was incorporated as a town. Its location, at the juncture of the Trent and Neuse rivers, brought steady growth. By 1774 it was capital of the province of North Carolina, complete with a grand and formal palace built by Royal Governor William Tryon. America's First Provincial Congress met at Tryon Palace in July 1774. The Georgian-style mansion was the governor's residence and statehouse, with assembly hall, council chamber and public offices. It included a kitchen house, a poultry house, a smokehouse and formal gardens. John Hawkes designed what was called "the most beautiful building in the Colonial Americas." The citizens of New Bern were not pleased with Tryon's extravagance. It was a time of discontent – the last hours before the American Revolution. Tryon's stay at the Palace was short-lived. He was transferred to New York, replaced by Josiah Marton who further offended the people by adding rooms to the mansion which they thought belonged in a London suburb.

Much later, at the turn of the century, Caleb Bradham, a New Bern druggist, brought a different kind of fame to New Bern by inventing Pepsi Cola.

North of New Bern on the mainland is Bath, North Carolina's oldest town, first official port of entry, and first meeting place of the colonial assembly of the Province. The town was settled beside the Pamlico River as early as 1690 and named for the Earl of Bath, one of the Lords Proprietors, in 1696.

Inland from Bath, on the Pamlico River, is Washington. The town's earliest records are dated October 1, 1776, making it the first town in the country to take this significant name. Edna Ferber visited the Jane Adams Floating Theater in Washington to gather information for *Showboat*. Although the locale for the book is the Mississippi River, she used Beaufort County names and copied verbatim an insccription in St. Thomas Church at Bath. Washington's tobacco warehouses are among many in eastern North Carolina where visitors are welcome from August to November. Others are in Rocky Mount, Wilson, Tarboro, Greenville, Williamston, Kinston, Goldsboro, Fayetteville, Lumbertown, Whiteville, and Smithfield. Wilson is the largest tobacco center in the state, leading the world in the production of flue-cured tobacco.

Originally produced only for export, tobacco was the State's first commercial crop. It was packed in huge hogsheads (barrels) and rolled through the woods to water-edge inspection houses where sailors broke open the casks for examination before bargaining. After a time, state supervisors inspected only the top layer, and poor quality tobacco was often "nested" underneath. Buyers would later discover that most of the tobacco was inferior. The looseleaf system of selling tobacco was born out of this corrupt practice. Sellers spread the leaves in loose piles and auctioned each pile in warehouses and in street sales.

An auctioneer's job is to get a fair market price for both farmer and buyer. The best of them can chant an incredible 500 words a minute. At a contest, auctioneers are judged on their smoothness and clarity, their ability to catch bids, settle disputes, close sales and move rapidly from pile to pile. An audience listens to the rapid chants for entertainment. It doesn't matter if they can't understand a word, feet tap to the lilting rhythms and the chanted beat. Watching the buyers is entertaining, too. On the opposite side of the rows of tobacco from the auctioneer, they move steadily, signalling their bids with a cock of the head, the crook of a finger or a twitch of the eyebrow. While the mouth moves faster than the eye can see, the auctioneer must watch every move of the buyers.

Edenton sits on the western shores of North Carolina's Albemarle Sound. Tucked far inside the Outer Banks, the town was once a thriving seaport. Shipbuilding was big business and merchants exported pitch, tar, turpentine, lumber, tobacco, corn, salt meat and fish. Incorporated in 1722, and named after Governor Charles Eden, this waterside village was North Carolina's capital until 1743. Through those years and up to the Revolution, its port cleared many boats loaded with goods for New England, Great Britain, and the West Indies. During the war, it remained a principal supply source for the colonies, and many locals distinguished themselves nationally as patriotic leaders. Joseph Hewes, a signer of the Declaration of Independence, James Iredell, associate justice of the first Supreme Court and Samuel Johnston, first United States Senator from North Carolina, were among those leaders.

In 1765 the British Parliament passed the Stamp Act as a way of taxing the colonists. Commissioners for each colony were appointed to sell the stamps, which would be attached to newspapers, college diplomas, legal papers, official documents, licenses to operate a business and many other pieces of paper. It would mean that an equivalent of a million dollars would be turned over to the British government each year. The colonists were furious and eventually effected a repeal of the Stamp Act in 1766. In 1773 Parliament came up with an idea to export tea into America, helping both England and the East India Company. They would reduce the price of tea to a ridiculous amount, with only a small duty, so that people would discard their objections to the tea tax. It didn't work quite as they planned. Eastern ports refused to let the tea ships dock. In Boston a group of citizens disguised as Indians boarded the ships and dumped the cargo into the harbor. Parliament retaliated by closing the Boston Port and moving the capital to Salem. North Carolinians came to the rescue by sending extensive provisions to Salem for the relief of Boston.

Soon after that 51 ladies from several counties met in Edenton to demonstrate their patriotism at what became known as the Edenton Tea Party. They signed and sent to England resolutions supporting the protest of the Provincial Congress against British injustice to the colonies.

Shad and herring fisheries have always been important to Edenton's economy, but its most important asset is the Jumbo peanut grown in the region's loamy soil. Edenton has the largest peanut market in the State and the second largest in the country.

Halifax County marks the northern divide between North Carolina's coastal plain and piedmont plateau. Halifax, founded in 1723 as the county seat, was called a "pretty town" and "considered among the most polished and cultivated in the State." A wedding in 1790 was celebrated by 22 consecutive dinner parties, in so many houses, the dinners being regularly succeeded by dances and all terminating in a great ball. But Halifax is celebrated for more than its social aplomb. It took the first official action by any Colonial legislature for absolute separation from Great Britain and for national independence. On April 12, 1776, Samuel Johnston, president of the Provincial Congress, with the delegates, authorized Joseph Hewes, William Hooper and John Penn as North Carolina's representatives to the Continental Congress. That resolve is noted on the North Carolina flag, which bears the date. April 12, Halifax Day, is a State holiday.

Fayetteville is south of Halifax, on the west bank of the Cape Fear River. The city was named for General Lafayette. For a few months in 1774 Fayetteville was the home of the famous Highland heroine Flora MacDonald. In her native Scotland she had saved Bonnie Prince Charlie from the British by allowing him to pose as her Irish maid, "Betty Burke." The disguise worked and the Prince was delivered into friendly hands. Thirty years later Flora MacDonald emigrated to North Carolina. A Fayetteville hero of more recent history, George Herman Ruth ("The Babe") hit his first home run in professional baseball while training with the Baltimare Orioles here in 1914.

Nearby are Pope Air Force Base and Fort Bragg, home of "The Airborne" as well as the Special Forces "Green Berets." The southern Piedmont's white sand and longleaf pine indicate an area known as the Sandhills. Pinehurst and Southern Pines, with 26 courses within a 15-mile radius, make Sandhills the winter golf capital of America. The oldest organized hunt in North Carolina, the Moore County Hounds, started at Southern Pines in 1814. Today, the Moore County Hounds turn out in traditional dress for fox and drag hunts between November and late March. Thoroughbreds and Standardbreds are trained for racing, and in April the Stoneybrook Steeplechase is a major event.

Research Triangle Park, the nation's largest corporate R.&D. center, is located on a gently rolling tract of 6300 acres in the eastern Carolina Piedmont. The park takes its name from the fact that it is nearly equidistant from the University of North Carolina in Chapel Hill, the State's first institution of higher learning, Duke University in Durham and Carolina State University in Raleigh. The three universities provide technical assistance and a broad spectrum of cultural activities. The communities offer distinctly different living styles. Chapel Hill is a small university town, not unlike Princeton, N.J.; Durham is an industrial city as well as a college town. Both cities are attractive to professionals. The largest population from Research Triangle Park lives in Raleigh, however.

The founders of RTP required that developments be on no less than eight acres and that no more than 15 percent of any tract of land be developed. The result is a park, not an industrial village. Stands of southern pine, oak andd hickory are occasionally interrupted by roads inconspicuously marked by signs like IBM, Data General, Airco, Becton Dickinson, Hercules, General Electric and TRW. Forty-seven Research and Development companies employ 24,000 people.

Duke University was established by a descendant of Washington Duke, a magnate of North Carolina's dominant industry – tobacco. Washington's son James B. (Buck) Duke was to tobacco what Rockefeller was to oil and Carnegie to steel.

Durham was only a tiny village when, in 1865, General Joseph E. Johnston surrendered to General W. T. Sherman a few miles west at Bennett House. That was the last major army of the Confederacy. At the end of the War Washington Duke walked 137 miles home to his tobacco farm. Duke began grinding tobacco, and by 1880, he and his three sons were making cigarettes. A few years later, with James B. Duke in command, machines were producing 100,000 cigarettes a day. The Duke family had a firm control of the U.S. tobacco industry when they formed the American Tobacco Company in 1911 and Durham was established as the world's tobacco capital. Fourteen years later Duke died, leaving an endowment of $80 million, the largest originating from the South. Duke University was the beneficiary of his name and a large portion of the endowment.

The University of North Carolina at Chapel Hill is the State's oldest institution of higher learning. It opened its doors in 1793 and created a community which has continued to lure playwrights, novelists, distinguished educators, scientists and artists. Thomas Wolfe began his literary career at the University of North Carolina.

About 15 miles north of Chapel Hill is historic Hillsborough, established in 1754 and once capital of the colony of North Carolina. Six of the Regulators whose uprising against the British ended in defeat at the Battle of Alamance on May 16, 1771 were hung in Hillsborough. Alamance battleground, five miles south of Burlington, is regarded by many historians as the site of the first major confict of the American Revolution.

Raleigh, North Carolina's capital, is on the eastern fringe of the Piedmont Plateau. The granite Capitol Building, of Greek Revival architecture, stands in a six-acre square. Among the monuments in the square is an equestrian statue honoring the three presidents born in North Carolina: Andrew Johnson, James K. Polk and Andrew Jackson. About one mile from Capitol Square is the Andrew Johnson House, a tiny, gambrel-roofed edifice where the 17th president was born.

Raleigh functions as a governmental, educational, commercial and social center. With six colleges, a historical museum, natural history museum, art galleries, a civic center, and musical associations including the North Carolina Symphony Orchestra, it enjoys a rich cultural life.

Some 19,000 people came to see Raleigh's new North Carolina Museum of Art open in 1982. The museum, decorated in the colors of earth, is set in a pastoral landscape on the outskirts of the city. The museum holds funerary arts from ancient Egypt, works of European masters and Classical Greek and Roman sculptures. One hallway portrays a history of America from colonial times through the early 20th century. Andrew Wyeth, Georgia O'Keffe and contemporary artists like Robert Rauschenberg have their place in the museum. A separate room is reserved for works by North Carolina artists.

The earliest settlers around Greensboro, west of Raleigh, were English and Welsh Quakers, German Calvinists and Lutherans, and Ulster Scottish Presbyterians. The town was named in honor of General Nathaneal Greene, commander of the colonial forces at nearby Guilford Courthouse in 1781. General George Cornwallis won a Pyrrhic victory at the battle of Guilford Courthouse on March 15. It proved to be the turning point of the Revolution in the South, setting the stage for the Battle of Yorktown the following fall which resulted in both the end of the war and in American independence.

In May, Sedgefield, a suburb of Greensboro, hosts one of the South's oldest horse shows. The Sedgefield Hunt season lasts from October until spring. William Sidney Porter, writer of short stories under the pen name "O. Henry," was born in Greensboro. The drugstore where he worked as a youngster has been reconstructed in the Greensboro Historical Museum. Since early times, textiles have played an important part in the city's economy. The first steam-powered cotton mill in North Carolina was built here in 1828.

In the north central Piedmont are High Point, Thomasville and Lexington. Skillfully crafted furniture is the main attraction in those cities and in hundreds of small factories along a 140-mile "furniture highway." The Southeastern Furniture Exposition Building at High Point hosts annual furniture markets, attended by buyers from throughout America and from abroad. North Carolina is the world's largest furniture manufacturer.

In cities and countryside the arts have flourished in North Carolina. With help from both public and private sectors, the state has received national applause for its standing in the arts. Since World War II the coalition of government, commerce and individuals has shaped that environment.

Along the way, North Carolina has secured some innovative firsts. In 1947 it appropriated public funds for an art collection. A state-supported school of the arts was created in 1963 and a cultural agency was placed in a cabinet position in 1971. The country's first local arts council was formed in 1949 in Winston-Salem. Today, there are 93 arts councils across North Carolina. In addition, the National Endowment for the Arts has used the town's urban arts program as a model for other cities.

The 1982 opening of the Roger L. Stevens Center for the

Performing Arts in Winston-Salem was similar to a Broadway premiere. A searchlight directed throngs to the center. They gathered on the sidewalk to applaud the nation's superstars of the arts as they stepped from limousines. Among them were conductor Leonard Bernstein, violinist Isaac Stern, choreographer Agnes DeMille and actors Cliff Robertson and Gregory Peck. Winston-Salem labeled it the social occasion of the year, and Gregory Peck called the town "a city of vigor."

Salem was founded in 1766 and Winston in 1849; the two towns consolidated in 1913. In 1752 the Moravian bishop, August G. Spangenberg, led a surveying party on horseback from Edenton to the Blue Ridge Mountains and down the Yadkin River Valley. Finally camping at the "three forks of Muddy Creek" in January 1753, Spangenberg wrote: "This is the best land we have found that is not yet taken in North Carolina.

The Moravians bought 98,985 acres of that land and called the tract "Wachau" after the ancestral Austrian estate of Count Zinzendorf, patron and cherished leader of the Moravian Church. The name became Wachovia. In October of that same year 12 Moravian men walked from Pennsylvania to Wachovia and lodged in a hunter's abandoned cabin at the edge of a meadow. While wolves howled in surrounding forests the small group "rejoiced heartily" during their first love feast or fellowship meeting in the provisional shelter. That settlement, named Bethabara, or House of Passage, was later called Old Town.

The Moravian Church, a Christian community founded in Bohemia, grew out of the reform movement of John Huss and was influenced by the teachings of John Wycliffe. The Moravian men who traveled from Pennsylvania to North Carolina were chosen for their religious conviction and skills for starting a new life. They were welcome in a frontier country that lacked ministers, doctors and capable craftsmen. The Moravians continued their customs, including New Year's Eve Watch Night, the love feasts and Easter Sunrise Service proclaiming Christ's triumph over the grave. They maintained their love of music by playing makeshift instruments such as a wooden trumpet carved from a hollowed tree limb. Later they brought in French horns, trombones, a violin and even an organ.

Before his death in 1760 Count Zinzendorf named the Wachovia tract Salem, which means "peace." The Revolutionary War conflicted with the beliefs of the peace-loving Moravians of North Carolina. As neutralists these German Protestants only wanted to be left alone. They aided the Patriots with supplies and shelter, but for the seven years of fighting they never took up arms. The peace they and everyone else wanted finally came at the Treaty of Paris in 1783. The next summer, the Moravians, in what is now Winston-Salem, gave thanks for the end of the war. The day was July 4, 1783, and some claim it as the first official July Fourth celebration in the country. Music aroused the town on that July morning, and the Moravians met in church for a traditional love feast which included prayer followed by buns and coffee. That night they gathered again, and in the quavering light of lantern and torch, marched around the square singing hymns.

Today, in the restored village of Old Salem, people still meet, often at night, for 18th-century Moravian music, prayer and torch-and-lantern processions. Each year, hundreds of visitors watch Old Salem flicker back in time to July 4, 1783. At 9 p.m., electric lights of houses facing the square are extinguished, and waves of candlelight glow in the windows. Singers in 18th-century dress emerge from houses carrying candle lanterns and kerosene torches. They join a Moravian church band in front of Main Hall at Salem College and begin to sing "Now Thank We All Our God."

Then the choir mixes with "townspeople." The men and boys in one group and the women and girls in another line up behind the band and march around the square singing "Jesus Make My heart Rejoice."

After a blessing the townspeople return to their homes, singing softly. The lights of lanterns and of candles in the windows vanish. The night watchman blows a single blare on a conch horn and cries out in the darkness, "Hear, brethren, hear; the hour of nine is come. Keep pure each heart and chaste every home." Immediately, electric lights beam again, bringing Old Salem back to the 20th century.

At the outbreak of the Civil War, the younger generation of Moravians, removed from the prohibition of bearing arms, enlisted with their neighbors. However, Wachovia saw Union soldiers only twice. After the war, the little town of Winston, twin to Salem, grew rapidly and soon became a center of industry. Salem had been known for the Nissen Wagon Works, founded in 1787, and the F. and H. Fries Woolen Mills, founded in 1840. However, over a period of time the two communitys' businesses shifted to Winston, leaving Salem as a primarily residential community.

Around the turn of the century two Winston families established what would become dominant industries. Founded in 1875 the R.J. Reynolds Tobacco Company developed into the largest cigarette manufacturing plant in the world. Camel, Cavalier and Winston Salem cigarettes and Prince Albert Smoking Tobacco are made in Winston-Salem.

The Hanes brothers sold their tobacco factory to Reynolds and set out in new directions. Pleasant Henderson Hanes began the P.H. Hanes Knitting Company in 1901, a giant in the manufacturing of men's and boys' knitwear. John Wesley Hanes founded the Hanes Hosiery Mills Company in 1900. Today it is the world's largest producer of women's nylon hosiery. Western Electric Company and Wachovia Bank and Trust Company, the largest bank between Washington and Atlanta, are also housed in Winston-Salem.

Charlotte, North Carolina's largest city, is situated on the southern end of the Piedmont Plateau. Named for Queen Charlotte of Mecklenburg, wife of England's George III, the "Queen City" has been preoccupied with commerce and industry since its inception. One-fourth of the nation's textile industry is in North Carolina, and Charlotte does nearly every kind of work in the field from spinning and weaving, dyeing and finishing, to making chemicals and textile machinery. Charlotte didn't get into the textile business until after the war between the States.

Long before that, in 1795, James J. Polk, 11th president of the United States, was born a short distance south of the city. At about the same time gold was discovered and Charlotte became the center of a gold rush. Until 1848, when gold was discovered in California, North Carolina was the leading gold producing state in the Union.

Today, Charlotte's handsome Coliseum, Ovens Auditorium and Merchandise Mart form a complex which holds sports and cultural events, trade fairs and expositions. The Mint Museum of Art has a superb collection of paintings and other art works. Near Charlotte is Motor Speedway, one of the region's major stock car tracks. Stock car racing was born in the South, and Motor Speedway draws more fans in May and October than California's Rose Bowl on New Year's Day.

The rolling hill country of the Piedmont, with stiff clay soils, many swift streams, and densely populated, meets the Blue Ridge Mountains, a part of the Appalachian chain. The steep, ragged Blue Ridge and Great Smoky Ranges reach their highest points in western North Carolina, and together they form the greatest mountain mass in the eastern half of the United States.

Brevard sits at the mountains' edge. Brevard Music Center celebrated its 48th season in 1984. For seven weeks, starting in June, musicians bring their talents to the Center. They range from seventh graders to veteran symphony performers. Those who come as students share their love of music in special public concerts. Musical notes float on airy breezes and waves of heat as trees shade students and teacher practicing bassoon, tuba or trombone. Each of Brevard's 340 students must join two or more of the center's 24 performing groups. They may participate in the opera program, perform in one of the three orchestras, two bands or many chamber ensembles.

Near Brevard is Flat Rock, where the home of Carl Sandburg has been appointed a National Historical Site. Fringing Flat Rock, Pisgah National Forest is the location of the first forestry school in America. The forest itself covers 479,232 acres.

Asheville, surrounded by the mountains, is the area's largest city. Asheville is a resort town and seat of Buncombe County. Buncombe is also spelled bunkum. The word "bunk," meaning anything said, written or done for mere show, originated with a speech by a Buncombe County Representative that was a masterpiece of fence-sitting. When asked the point of his speech he answered, "I was just talking for Buncombe." Ashville's boarding house at 48 Spruce Street is the Thomas Wolfe Memorial, "Dixieland" in the town's famous native son's first novel, *Look Homeward Angel*. The former family home has the same furnishings and possessions as when Wolfe's mother opened it to paying guests. Another Asheville area home has opened its doors to paying guests, but as tourists rather than boarders.

In the year 1887, Commodore Vanderbilt's grandson George Washington Vanderbilt decided he wanted to live in the most luxurious country estate in America. He chose a 125,000 acre site on the outskirts of Asheville where he could indulge in a panoramic view of a broad river valley and the Blue Ridge mountains. Because of its reputed pure air Asheville was already a fashionable resort town for well-to-do health seekers. Young Vanderbilt hired Richard Morris Hunt, the most acclaimed architect of the time, to create a chateau. Eight years and an estimated $5 million later, he became the proud owner of Biltmore House. The grounds and gardens are the work of America's greatest landscape architect, Frederick Law Olmsted.

Vanderbilt's new home turned out to be an early 16th-century French Château, complete with turrets and pinnacles, but with central heating, electric lights and functional iron beams. A view of Biltmore House, set in the center of 8,000 acres, is postponed by a three-mile approach. The road, designed for horsedrawn carriages, was intended to create "the sensation of passing through the remote depths of a natural forest," Olmsted told Vanderbilt. A lush forest of trees bedecked with vines, a small river running near the road, and tropical plantings, give the feeling of being in a southern wilderness. "People coming from New York to Biltmore in the winter or spring must be made to feel they are decidedly nearer the sun," Olmsted said.

At the end of the shady, secluded road is an iron-barred gate. The chateau is still hidden from view. A visitor must turn sharply to the right before he sees turrets competing with mountain tops. A long, formal courtyard leading to Biltmore House contrasts with the wildness of the woods. Though the château dominates the landscape it is not massive. Hunt recreated the graceful Renaissance-style palaces of the Loire Valley. A Château de Blois is certainly better suited in an Appalachian river valley than along Fifth Avenue, where other Vanderbilt mansions were found. Hunt said about George Vanderbilt's carefully-chosen site, "The mountains are just the right size and scale for the château." He developed an interchange between Biltmore House and

Olmsted's rolling meadows and parkland by placing windows in every room. Featured are the faraway hazy blue mountains of Pisgah National Forest.

The main upstairs rooms at Biltmore are open to visitors year around and include the entrance hall, salons, elegant bedrooms and adjoining balconies, the library, an oak-panelled sitting room and a sky-lit "palm court" – Vanderbilt's handsome red-and-walnut bedroom. The kitchens, pantries and servants' hall in the vast 50-room basement; the banquet hall with its rows of chairs against a long table and side walls, and a 70-foot ceiling, and a number of rooms with magnificent fireplaces are all on display.

Parts of the chateau illustrate a vanished time. Besides the living quarters for 80 servants there is a "bachelor's wing" invented by Victorians. The wing includes the billiard room, the smoking room and the trophy room. Above them are the bachelor bedrooms so the men could go from after-dinner billiards to bed without the least risk of meeting a female guest during illicit evening hours.

Contrary to accepted opinion, George Vanderbilt's purse was not bottomless. He died in 1914 and in 1930 his hard-pressed widow opened Biltmore to a paying public. Today, Biltmore is owned by a Vanderbilt grandson. It is still the price of the admission tickets that keeps the place so splendidly preserved. What was built by a multi-millionaire has been saved by sightseers.

To the west of Asheville the Great Smoky Mountains rise to dramatic heights. A hiker deep in the Smokies, swallowed by mountain and forest, finds his world diminished to the path before him. Grandiose sights surround him as he wends his way on the Appalachian Trail through the 800-square-mile Great Smoky Mountain National Park, but for the most part he is aware only of his immediate environment. That environment is magnificent. Myriad trees, from lowland gums and magnolias to ridgetop conifers, form a green, canopied tunnel. Growing in their shade are some 1,300 varieties of flowering plants, 350 mosses and liverworts, 230 lichens and 2,000 kinds of fungus.

A billion to 600 million years ago the present site of the Smokies was an arm of the ocean. Then, about 230 million years ago, great convulsions shook the earth causing it to crack, buckle and twist. A new mountain system was born. Called the Appalachian Revolution by geologists, these cataclysmic forces formed the Appalachian chain, leaving the Smokies in their present position. Glaciers stripped away much of the rich soil in New England but stopped at the Ohio River. The Canadian-zone flora and fauna, retreating before the great ice masses, established new footholds in the Smokies where they still survive. Because it is the meeting ground of northern and southern forests, there are more than 150 kinds of trees now growing in the Smoky Mountains.

The Smokies get as much as 100 inches of rain a year, forming a flawless greenhouse. In the summer the rain is soft and warm – a mere spray. It sprinkles the air with smells of new life in the woods. Summer-blooming herbs, mosses and dwarfed rose-pink Carolina rhododendron, the "deer laurel" that grows in the southern mountains, and nowhere else, are surrounded by a rolling haze. A towhee flicks her long, rounded tail near her nest in a spruce or fir. Tiny winter wrens make their presence known with melodious, high-pitched trilling. "There is not a cranny in the rocks of the Great Smokies, not a foot of the wild glen, but harbors something lovable and rare," wrote Kephart, outdoorsman and author, who moved to what would become his beloved mountains. Kephart also wrote, "It is not the clearing but the unfenced wilderness that is the camper's real home... I love the unimproved works of God."

The unimproved works of God are everywhere in the Smoky Mountains. Blackberry bushes, holly, dogwood, sassafras, grapevine, sumac, dog hobble, leucothoe and groves of white pine and hemlock fill the woods. Before the park was established in 1934, and officially dedicated by President Franklin Delano Roosevelt six years later, there were little back-country settlements of hewn-log dwellings. Germans from Pennsylvania, Scotch-Irish from the Carolinas, and English from Tidewater, Virginia came after the French and Indian War ended in 1763. They set up logging camps, logging railroads and raised herds of cattle which grazed on the grassy mountaintops. Reminders of those days remain, but for the most part those areas coalesce with the portions of the park that were never cultivated and where trees were never cut. Professor Asa Cray, prominent Harvard botanist, once said that he encountered more species of trees within the 30 miles west of Asheville, North Carolina, than could be seen anywhere from the coast to the Rocky Mountains or in traveling from England clear across Europe to Turkey.

Great Smoky Mountains National Park, covering more than half a million acres, is tenant to some of the oldest mountains on earth. The highest mountain mass in eastern America, they rise for 70 miles astride the North Carolina-Tennessee border. At 6,643 feet Clingman's Dome, the tallest peak, stands as a fortress over the park.

The Smokies escaped the icy fingers of glaciers, giving sanctuary to many species of plant life. There are 50 different kinds of lily, 22 kinds of violets. White dogwood and trillium, purple dwarf mountain iris and red and yellow columbine purvey a kaleidoscope of color in the spring. Then, white and rose mountain laurel, thickets of azaleas varying from pure white to pink, yellow, and deep red and purple, pink and white rhododendrons add their beauty to "the unimproved works of God." Along streams lined with rhododendron grow towering hemlock, 400-year-old tulip poplars, black cherry, and white ash. The tulip poplar is a favourite tree of the southern hardwood forest. It belongs to the magnolia family and produces a tulip-like flower that can grow to 190 feet with a diameter of eight to ten feet.

The land for the Great Smoky Mountains National Park has been paid for and presented to the government by the people of Tennessee and North Carolina and by $5 million in matching funds donated by John D. Rockefeller, Jr., as a living memorial to his mother.

The splendor of the Smokies is appreciated, as evidenced by the large number of backpackers who roam its trails yearly. Black bears roam the Smokies in considerable numbers too. There are an estimated 350 within the park. They don't bother campers, but handouts are understandably prohibited. A bear may become lazy and unable to forage for himself. Beyond that his behaviour is unpredictable, particularly when he is hungry.

Although the black bear is the smallest of North American bears, he is strong. They generally live more than 15 years and weigh between 200 and 300 pounds. Their eyesight isn't well developed, but their senses of smell and hearing are. This omnivorous animal has a varied diet of rodents, reptiles, amphibians, fish, carrion and vegetable food. Honey is a favorite; a bear will eat his fill from a bee tree, crying pathetically from the stings on his vulnerable face. Bears don't truly hibernate. They put on extra fat in the fall and sleep through most of the cold winter, but they are easily awakened. When a bear emerges from his den in the spring, he searches for food. In early summer he sheds his winter coat and finds a mate. The next January or February a cub is born – twins are not uncommon. At birth, the blind, toothless, nearly hairless cub measures under a foot long and weighs less than a pound. He spends a year and a half with his mother, avoiding the father, who may turn cannibal if food is scarce.

Despite their strength, bears are not bold. They generally stay in the back country, so hikers on the Smoky's trails seldom see one.

The main route through the Park is Newfound Gap Road, which enters at Gatlinburg on the Tennessee side and at Cherokee on the North Carolina side. The eastern Cherokee were the first to call the Great Smoky Mountains home. To the Indians, the mountains reigned over "Shaconage" – place of blue smoke. In their legends, the Smokies had existed since the beginning of time, when a huge buzzard flew over the new earth, digging deep valleys and forming the rounded mountain peaks by raising his wings. The Cherokee built their villages on southern and western slopes. They lived in solid, grass-roofed houses with walls of upright poles covered with clay. In fertile valleys they planted corn, beans, pumpkins and squash. Their democratic nation stretched from the base of the sacred mountains to the dense pine forest hundreds of miles to the south. Hernando de Soto came upon the Cherokee in 1540, and found them to be a quiet, agricultural people governed by a loosely-structured tribal organization.

The Cherokee sided with the British against the colonists during the American Revolution, but after signing a treaty in 1785 with the new Government they changed their allegiance. In the war of 1812, Cherokee braves fought alongside Maj. Gen. Andrew Jackson and the Americans. In 1827 the Cherokee established their sovereignty. They adopted a constitution, collected taxes for roads and schools, discouraged intemperance and polygamy, and prohibited the selling of land to white men. The United States recognized their government.

Sequoya, an illiterate silversmith who had been crippled in a hunting accident, became fascinated by the white man's ability to "talk on paper." After years of solitary work he created a Cherokee alphabet with 85 letters, one for each syllable in the spoken language. A cherokee child could learn it in a matter of months. For more than a decade the Cherokee civilization prospered. Its boats carried its cotton to New Orleans for trade; its farms produced cows, horses, sheep, goats and hogs; the women made butter and cheese and wove cloth from cotton and wool. Cherokee owned inns, maintained their roads, and for the most part, they knew how to read and write. They even established a newspaper in 1828 – the *Cherokee Phoenix*. Then Benjamin Parks stumbled upon his golden nugget in the Indians' land. The Cherokee's laws and customs were abrogated and, in the end, they were forced to move.

In the summer of 1838, 5,000 Cherokee left their land. In the fall, another 13,000 set out, escorted by the United States army. One of the soldiers wrote: "On the morning of November 17th we encountered a terrific sleet and snow storm with freezing temperatures and from that day until we reached the end of the fateful journey on March the 26th 1839, the sufferings of the Cherokee were awful. The trail of the exiles was a trail of death. They had to sleep in the wagons and on the ground without fire. And I have known as many as twenty-two of them to die in one night of pneumonia due to ill treatment, cold, and exposure." In all, 4,000 died. The Cherokee called it the Trail of Tears.

About a thousand fled when the roundup began. In return for one of the number who was wanted for murder, General Scott let them stay. Today that remnant populates the eastern foothills of the Smokies. The reservation's main settlement is in the town of Cherokee, North Carolina. Curio shops line the main street catering for souvenir-seekers. Wide-eyed children clutch toy tepees, plastic bears and bows and arrows. Authentic Cherokee art and craft items are on display too. The baskets are intricately woven of white oak, river cane, and honeysuckle vines with designs made from vegetable and root dyes. Many of the carvings represent animals of the region, especially bears, foxes and opossums.

The Cherokee, with some variations, are returning to the days before Benjamin Parks and the gold rush. Though they can't sell to white men they own all the land on the reservation and have established a 12-member council plus a chief and vice chief. The tribe of 5,000 has a police force and fire department, and the schools are starting to teach the Cherokee language again. Teenage boys play drums and demonstrate traditional dances and men, women and children all participate in a more up-to-date dance called "clogging." They whirl and stomp while a drummer and guitarists with amplifiers thump out country tunes. They dance long into the night.

Oldtime music, played in Southern mountains, began a couple of generations ago when men were bound to the land. The tunes, the tempos and the traditions have survived to accompany stories of the backwoodsmen's way of life. When chores were done, the music began. They tapped their toes to the sounds of fiddle, banjo, dulcimer and later the guitar. Music became as much a part of their living as the mountains that defined their world. It was the catharsis for hard times.

Young people learned the music from their parents or neighbors, and families handed down their roughly-fashioned instruments as prized treasures. Then, in the 1920s and 1930s, radio replaced mountain music. The sound was packaged as Bluegrass up-tempoed tunes, and country-western made it a commercial success. Still, remnants of the oldtime music remain. Though the traditional musicians are fewer, the music persists and is played on porches, at square dances, and midnight suppers, throughout the mountain country.

The music varies from place to place, and is as rough-hewn and frayed around the edges as some of the instruments it is played on. With his father's help a young boy made a banjo out of wood, a piece of bucket, cut-up washtub and the bullet-marked hide of a rabbit. A woman strums a banjo which her brother made from a 1956 Buick transmission.

The banjo came to the South with West African black slaves. Americans added a fifth string in the early 1800s. The banjo is played today with the three-finger, rolling style usually associated with Bluegrass music. Oldtime, though, has different styles with a variety of names to describe them. Clawhammer, drop-thumb, flying-hand and frailing all evolved from the original stroke style, that of striking down on the strings, rather than picking upward.

Guitars came to oldtime music after World War I. At first it furnished back-up chords for the fiddle, then it began to star on its own. One boy started playing the guitar when he was 7 years old. He and his brothers would go "serenading" from house to house. To show their appreciation neighbors gave them a piece of pie or cake or another treat. Some young people have formed groups and perform regularly, and one guitarist alternates between playing guitar and spoons which he slaps in a rhythmical pattern.

Sounds of the dulcimer echo through Southern mountains too. The hammered dulcimer, with an exotic resonance, originated in Persia. You strike the box-like instrument's strings with small hammers. More familiar in the mountains is the lap dulcimer, brought across the Atlantic by the first settlers. It soon earned the name Appalachian dulcimer because of its popularity in that region. People held the instrument flat on their laps and plucked the three strings with a goose quill. Today they have more strings, and some folk strum and pick them like guitars. Old-line players just don't take to that. The traditional dulcimers are slim and light, often made with poplar sides, a pine neck and regular old wood paneling on the backs with diamond-shaped sound holes. They are strummed with a piece of cow's horn whittled into a pick.

Oldtime isn't oldtime without the fiddler and his bow. Just ask any mountain musician. The fiddle sailed to America in the 1600s, and year after year it has taken center stage for oldtime music. The fiddler pulls native pieces and Celtic tunes from his bow. He learned his music by ear and plays primarily to entertain himself. But the smiles on listeners' faces prove that the enjoyment spills over.

Oldtime musicians still play on the back porches of the South, but they're also moving to larger spaces where larger audiences gather. There are annual fiddlers' conventions, contests and festivals. Sometimes, entire towns are involved. Groups gather along streets, in front of shops for a good old jamboree. They bring their own folding chairs, sit in a close circle, and swap names of songs. Anyone can play. There are no rules. An appreciation of music is the only prerequisite. Many don't even play the instruments; they just come to listen and clap time. A guitar sets the rhythm, a banjo follows, then the fiddle takes the lead. They look into each other's eyes and take turns playing solos. For a brief time, someone may sing about the hard life, but the happy tunes always pick up again.

There are sanctuaries for this well-loved music. The Carter Family Fold (of Carter Family fame) has a stage, wooden benches covered with mix-and-match carpet pieces to seat 900, and a dance floor where several stomping feet keep time to the music. When a hoedown tune begins, the benches empty. Young dance with old as feelings of good will towards all permeate the space. Oldtime music will be around for a long time.

In the foothills town of Morganton, north of Asheville, lives Sam Irvin, a U.S. Senator for twenty years, and chairman of the Watergate hearings. Irvin lives about 200 feet from where he was born 87 years ago. Morganton fringes the Pisgah National Forest and is near Mount Mitchell which, at 6,684 feet, is the highest mountain east of the Mississippi River, and one of 49 peaks in North Carolina reaching 6,000 feet or more.

The towns of Boone, Blowing Rock and Banner Elk, surrounded by several ski areas, form a winter sports center. The town of Blowing Rock is named for a formation which has air currents swirling upward around it.

Many North Carolina toymakers belong to crafts guilds that sell members' work in guild shops and shows. One group is Blue Ridge Hearthside Crafts Cooperative in Boone. This organization has more than 350 crafts people making toys in their homes, workshops and on front porches. It began as a community action program with grants to help mountain people preserve their folk customs and ways. The group has been self-supporting for several years, giving employment to many who learned their toy-making skills from parents and grandparents. Shows are held in July, August and October.

To make a toy today, an artisan roughs out the shape with a power-saw then picks up a knife to finish the job. He fashions the traditional toys such as lumber jacks, pecking chickens, bouncing pigs and creates a few of his own. One man from Deep Gap made what he called a "walking mule," a crank toy with a farmer and a mule in harness. A turn of the crank moves the farmer's hands and plow lines and makes the mule walk, swish his tail and flop his ears. The Deep Gap man's works have been showcased in folk festivals in Washington D.C.

With an inherent love for the soil, North Carolina families have clung to their farms, while factories have risen beside them with unexpected grace. Nicknamed "Tar Heels" because of the early trade in pitch, turpentine and tar, North Carolina remains a small-town state of about 5.5 million people. From Cape Hatteras to the Great Smoky Mountains North Carolinians are obsessively loyal and to some "a bit too proud of not being proud." Stubborn independence has marked the Tar Heel State since it became the first colony to break with Great Britain and the last to secede from the Union. Still, it lost more men in the Civil War than any other Southern state.

Though one of the most rural states, North Carolina is becoming one of the most industrialized. Fishermen harvest nearly 17 million dollars' worth of edible fish annually from the coastal waters of the Outer Banks. Half a billion pounds of sweet potatoes are produced a year, and nearly as many pounds of peanuts. Poultry and hogs are big money-makers, but tobacco is still king. It brings in more than a billion dollars a year. Science and industry have reshaped the central Piedmont Plateau with Research Triangle Park, and a three-billion-dollar-a-year textile industry and unparalleled sales of wooden furniture. In the heart of rolling, wooded hills, the swath of industry and manufacturing from Charlotte to Raleigh symbolizes the New South. North Carolinians have a right to be proud of being proud.

Facing page: the Blue Ridge Mountains south of Asheville.

Previous pages: (left) the State Legislative Building and (right) St. Mary's College. These pages: (left) Legislative Building; (below and facing page) the graceful, Doric-style State Capitol; (bottom left) the Coliseum and State Fairgrounds and (bottom right) the downtown area, all in Raleigh.

Raleigh: (top left) the delicate fountains on Bicentennial Plaza; (top right) the Radisson Plaza Hotel on Fayetteville Street (above and right); (facing page) the imposing Doric portico of the State Capitol, which has been restored to its original 1840 appearance.

Raleigh: (top left) the State Fair held annually in October; (left) the State Capitol in its six acres of grounds; (above) the State Legislative Building, constructed in marble and granite to a design by Edward Durrell Stone, and (facing page) the Sovernor Mansion with the verandahs which are so common to the older buildings of the city.

Raleigh: (below) a peaceful waterway in Pullen Park; (right) the
Legislative Building; (bottom left) the Clock Tower at the State
University; (bottom right) Smedes Residence Hall at St. Mary's College and
(facing page) a farm near the airport.

27

Left: bales of hay await collection on a farm east of Silver City. Below: vintage cars in the Greensboro Historical Museum. Bottom left and overleaf left: golf at Greensboro. Bottom right: the North Carolina Zoological Park at Asheboro. Facing page: the Concord United Methodist Church. Overleaf right: costumed enthusiasts parade before re-enacting the Battle of Guilford Courthouse, which took place near Greensboro in 1781.

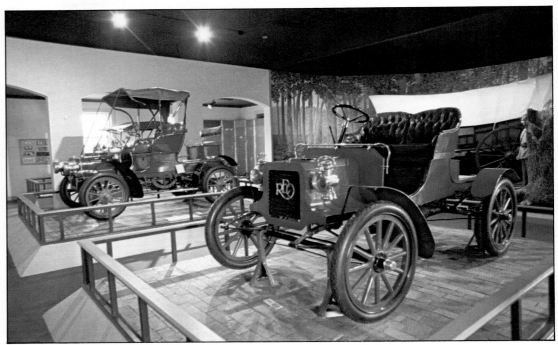

Winston-Salem: Reynolda House (top right), with its surrounding village (remaining pictures), was constructed as a model settlement in eclectic taste by the namesake and founder of the R.J. Reynolds Tobacco Company while the First World War raged in Europe. It is now open to the public.

Salem College, established in 1772, in Old Salem, a town built by Moravians in the 18th century as a congregation town: (left, bottom left and bottom right) the college campus; (below) Church Street; (facing page) the Howard Rondthaler Science Building and (overleaf) housing on Main Street.

Old Salem: (facing page, right and top right) housing on Main Street; (above) West Street and (top left) the Town Hall and Fire Station at the corner of Liberty and Cemetery. After the close of the Second World War many of these buildings were restored to their original condition.

Neither a massive rebuilding, nor a collection of structures from other sites, Old Salem is a genuine community which retains much of the refinement and elegance of the 18th century: (this page) houses on Main Street and (facing page) the Home Moravian Church, built in 1800.

Winston-Salem is the fourth largest city in the state and contains some of the most interesting architecture: (facing page) Winston Square; (left) Old Salem; (bottom left) First Baptist Church on Fifth Street; (bottom right) Smith Reynolds Library and (below) Graylyn Conference Center, both on Wake Forest University Campus, and (overleaf) the downtown area from the west.

Top left: an abandoned farmhouse near Mount Airy. Above: the granite dome that is the main feature of Stone Mountain State Park, near Roaring Gap. Top right: a bluegrass fiddler at Mount Airy. Right: a peaceful rural home near Mount Airy. Facing page: the Brinegar Cabin, where that family wove cloth between 1885 and 1935. Overleaf: scenes in Doughton Park.

Below: the majestic sight of Grandfather Mountain, near Linville. Bottom right: the Green Park Inn at Blowing Rock. Right and facing page: King Street in Boone, a town named for Daniel Boone who once camped here. Overleaf: the graceful manor house at the Moses Cone Memorial Park.

Hot air ballooning (these pages) is one of the more exhilerating sports in North Carolina. Overleaf: (left) the spectacular drop of Linville Falls and (right) the view from the Blue Ridge Parkway, south of Asheville.

In 1895 work was completed on Biltmore House (these pages). Built for George Vanderbilt as an American counterpart of the European 'working estate', Biltmore is now open to the public and displays the various processes of winemaking as well as the magnificent house.

Asheville: (above) the Thomas Wolfe Memorial, refurbished as it was in the days of his childhood; (top left) the fine Grove Park Inn; (facing page) the columned Buncombe County Courthouse and the City Building. Top right: the home of Carl Sandburg at Flat Rock. Right: the Craggy Gardens near Asheville. Overleaf: (left) a delicate waterfall in the Pisgah National Forest and (right) the Henderson County Courthouse in Hendersonville.

Above and facing page: Sliding Rock, where the Looking Glass Creek flows over a smooth rockface, giving endless fun for summer swimmers. Right: a Cherokee at the Oconaluftee Indian Village. Bottom right: a wooden house in the depths of the Pisgah National Forest. Top right: a flag flies atop the dramatic outcrop of Chimney Rock. This granite column towers 225 feet into the air and commands views of over 75 miles.

Once a Confederate naval base, Charlotte has become a bustling, modern center of trade and industry: (above, top left and facing page) the city from James B. Marshall Park; (right) the Convention Center with the Radisson Plaza Hotel beyond and (top right) Trade Street.

Charlotte: (left) a startling modern sculpture in Independence Square; (bottom left) Mecklenburg County Courthouse; (below) exciting action at the Charlotte Motor Speedway and (facing page) the original design of Independence Center on Trade Street.

Located at the head of navigation on the Cape Fear River, Fayetteville is the state's furthest inland port: (above) a fountain in pedestrianized Hay Street and (top left, left and facing page) the Market House, built in 1838 with an open first floor where local farmers could sell produce.

Once the largest city in the state, Wilmington was named for an English nobleman in 1734: (top left) the Thalian Hall of 1858; (above) Market Street; (right and facing page) Chandler's Wharf, an area of restored buildings dating back to the 1850s, and (top right) Front Street.

Wilmington: (top left) a replica of the Statue of Liberty; (above) the Governor Dudley Mansion of 1825, now the center of the Historic Wilmington Foundation; (right) the Memorial Water Gardens; (top right) Orton Plantation, built in 1740, and (facing page) Poplar Grove Plantation.

When the *USS North Carolina* (these pages and overleaf) steamed into service soon after Pearl Harbour she was the most powerful battleship ever sent to sea by the United States. She now lies at Wilmington as a memorial to the thousands of North Carolinians who died in World War II.

The Cape Fear River: (facing page) the *John Taxis*, built in 1869 and the oldest tugboat in America; (above) downtown Wilmington and the I.17 roadbridge; (top left) the *USS North Carolina*; (right and top right) moored tugboats. Overleaf: Southport, near the mouth of the Cape Fear River.

The low, sandy islands and peninsulas around Cape Fear: (facing page, below and overleaf left) Caswell Beach; (right and overleaf right) the harbor at Southport; (bottom left) Southport Town Pier and (bottom right) Caswell Beach Lighthouse.

Above and top right: part of the large hire fleet at Swansboro, at the mouth of the White Oak River. Top left, left and facing page: Morehead City, from where many fishing boats put out to troll the waters of Brogue Sound.

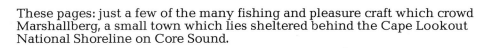

These pages: just a few of the many fishing and pleasure craft which crowd Marshallberg, a small town which lies sheltered behind the Cape Lookout National Shoreline on Core Sound.

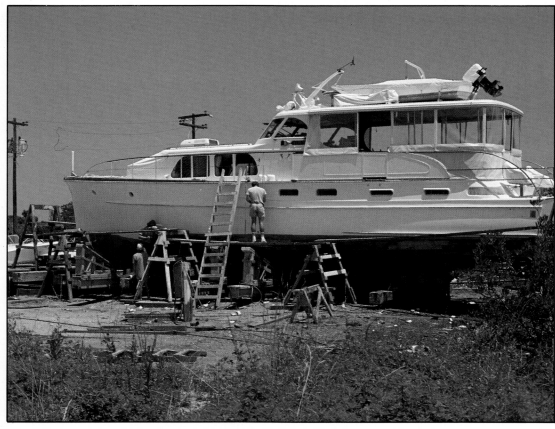

These pages: the magnificent sandy beaches around Fort Macon, where North Carolinians come to bathe, fish or otherwise enjoy themselves.

Fort Macon (these pages) was completed in 1834 as a coastal defence work and is a fine example of an early-19th-century fortress. Garrisoned by North Carolina, it fell to Unionists in 1862 and was abandoned soon after the war, though it was pressed back into service during World War II.

New Bern, second oldest city in the state: (top left) Municipal Building; (left) George Street; (above) Catholic Church on Middle Street. Facing page: views on the waterfront: (top left) a fine home; (top right) a small ship; (bottom left) fishing and (bottom right) the city from the River Trent. Overleaf: (left) a Corinthian-columned home on the waterfront and (right) a house on George Street.

These pages: Tryon Palace, a magnificent recreation of the 18th century governor's mansion, where both colonial and state governments met: (left) the kitchen garden; (below and bottom right) the stables and (bottom left and facing page) the main house and 18th-century style gardens.

Tryon Palace at New Bern: (facing page) the formal gardens in the style so popular when the original palace was built in 1767; (above) costumed museum staff outside the palace; (top right) the dining room and (right) the exterior of the rebuilt palace.

Along the low-lying coasts of Pamlico County are many small fishing towns, among them: (facing page and bottom right) Oriental, with its many-sparred fishing craft and (left, bottom left and below) Minnesott, with its long, wooden jetty and small ferry boat.

Manteo, one of the largest towns on Roanoke Island: (top left) Dare County Courthouse; (top right and overleaf left) Sir Walter Raleigh Street; (left, facing page and overleaf right) the waterfront and (above) the Lost Colony Theatre, where events surrounding the disappearence of Raleigh's Roanoke colony in the 1580s are re-enacted.

Above: a scene from a performance at the Lost Colony Theatre in Manteo. Remaining pictures and overleaf: Manteo's *Elizabeth II*, a 69-foot-long replica of a 50-tunne bark of the type used to bring colonists to Roanoke Island during the 16th century.

These pages: the Sunken Garden, a part of the Elizabethan Gardens, north of
Manteo. The gardens were planted in 1951 by the Garden Club of North
Carolina as a memorial to the first English Colonists.

Below: a replica of the *Kittyhawk,* the first successful powered aircraft, in the Wright Brothers National Memorial at Kitty Hawk. Right and overleaf right: Pirates Cove Marina. Bottom left: the "Ghost Ship" at Nags Head. Bottom right: colorful catamarans at Nags Head. Facing page: a building at Nags Head which is raised on stilts as protection against the waves. Overleaf left: dusk at Manteo.

Facing page and bottom right: the distinctive, spiral paint scheme of Cape Hatteras Lighthouse, which warns of the Diamond Shoals. Below: Nags Head Beach. Right: Charles Creek and (bottom left and overleaf right) a magnificent home on East Main Street, both in Elizabeth City. Overleaf left: boats on the Pasquotank River.

These pages: houses and early-morning fishermen along Nags Head Beach. Overleaf: (left) Oregon Inlet on Bodie Island and (right) Bodie Island Lighthouse on Roanoke Sound.

INDEX